D1557957

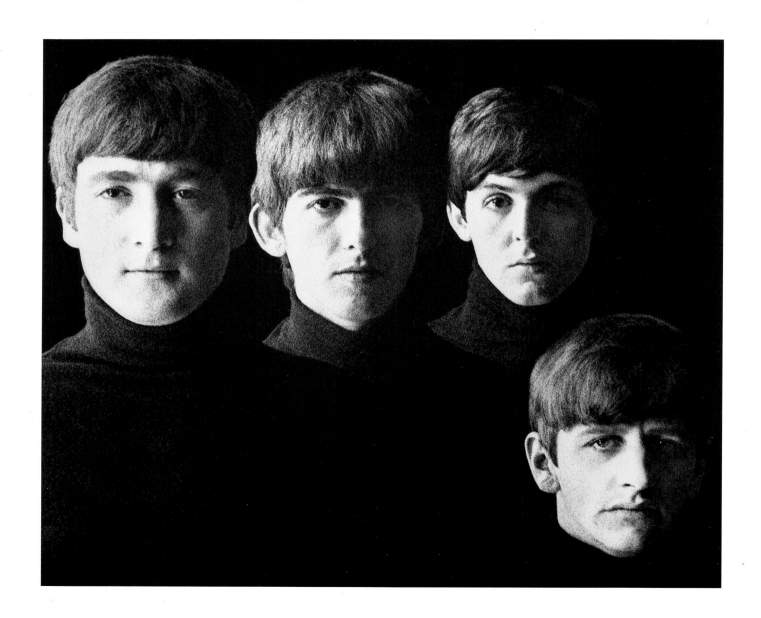

YESTERDAY

THE BEATLES 1963-1965
ROBERT FREEMAN

FOREWORD BY PAUL McCARTNEY

HOLT RINEHART AND WINSTON/NEW YORK

To John, Paul, George, Ringo and Tiddy

PAGE 1 Ringo Starr, 1963.
FRONTISPIECE The Beatles. The photo was used for the album cover of
'Meet The Beatles'. 1963.

Foreword copyright © 1983 MPL Ltd
Photographs, text and captions copyright © 1983 Robert Freeman

Published in the United States by Holt, Rinehart and Winston,
383 Madison Avenue, New York, New York 10017

Originally published in Great Britain under the title *Yesterday:
Photographs of the Beatles*

Library of Congress Cataloging in Publication Data
Freeman, Robert, 1936–
Yesterday: the Beatles, 1963–1965.
1. Beatles—Iconography.   I. Title.
ML421.B4F73   1983   784.5'4'00922 [B]   83–8504
ISBN:0–03–064033–4

First American Edition
Original book design by Robert Freeman
Design and typography by Sara Komar
Printed in Italy

1 3 5 7 9 10 8 6 4 2

FOREWORD

When Bob Freeman first took photographs of the Beatles, we treated him like any other photographer. It was when he returned with the results that we began to look at him in a different light. He brought with him large grainy prints, the like of which we had never seen before.

Being given these made a great impression on us, and consequently we were eager to pose for him from then on. Although many other people were taking photos of us at that time, I think we all felt that his stuff somehow summed up our own feelings.

The photographs were artistic without being pretentious, and yet they were commercial enough to be enjoyed by the ordinary fan in the street. The fact that we always felt quite easy about being snapped by him shows in the pictures themselves.

When we came to choose which of Bob's photos we should use for the cover of 'Rubber Soul', he visited us at a friend's flat one evening. Whilst projecting the slides on to an album-sized piece of white cardboard, Bob inadvertently tilted the card backwards. The effect was to stretch the perspective and elongate the faces. We excitedly asked him if it was possible to print the photo in this way. Being Bob, he said 'yes', and the cover to our album 'Rubber Soul' was decided.

I have a feeling that his photos were amongst the best ever taken of the Beatles.

PAUL MCCARTNEY

5

The Beatles' boots.

WITH THE BEATLES · 1963 - 1965

In the summer of 1963 I went to Bournemouth, on the south coast of England, to meet the Beatles, who were then in the middle of their first nationwide tour. What began as a two- or three-day photographic assignment led to a professional association lasting for several years.

My interest in the Beatles came about through a friend of mine who had seen them play at the Cavern Club in Liverpool and had subsequently filmed them for TV. Through a press agent I contacted their manager, Brian Epstein, at Rhyl in North Wales, where the group were working their way south on tour, and he asked me to send samples of my work. I sent him some photos of jazz musicians, among them John Coltrane, which I had taken the previous year. A few days later Brian phoned me to say that they all liked the photographs and he suggested that I meet them in Bournemouth the following week.

Bournemouth is a respectable resort town where elderly people retire for some peace and quiet. Not the most likely place to meet the Beatles, but Brian Epstein, with his discreet charm, was not the sort of figure one would expect to be an entrepreneur of popular music. When I met him in the hotel lobby he was courteous and soft-spoken. Although from Liverpool, he had the accent and manners of a Knightsbridge man. We went up to the coffee lounge to wait for the Beatles. George Harrison was already there, reading a newspaper in a large comfortable armchair. He too greeted me in a friendly fashion but, unlike Brian, with a rich Liverpool accent. Then the other three Beatles arrived: George's dry humour was counterpointed by Paul's breezy manner, John's slightly reserved air and Ringo's jauntiness. As a group they generated warmth and good humour. They all wore similar dark-toned clothes – wool turtlenecks and worsted trousers – with pointed black boots, and they spoke with varying Liverpool accents. They seemed relaxed in their relationship to Brian, but their respect was laced with a mischievous irreverence: they called him 'Eppy', while he referred to them as 'the boys'.

That evening I experienced, for the first time, the Beatles' music live onstage.

They were playing at a cinema down the street from the hotel and already their movements were monitored by a rising swell of fans that was to become the great wave of Beatlemania. Brian had arranged a position for me near the stage and escorted me down the aisle with a smile that registered the excitement of the audience, nearly all girls in their early teens. During the opening act, which was interrupted by repeated screams for the Beatles, I decided to go backstage and catch some of the pre-performance atmosphere.

I began taking my first photographs in the small dressing room occupied by the Beatles and their immediate entourage, which included Neil Aspinall, their road manager, Tony Barrow, their press agent, and John's wife, Cynthia, who sat quietly on a bench in the corner next to John while he tuned his guitar. Paul read fan mail and signed autographs, George munched on a sandwich and Ringo sat with his leg over a chair — watching and waiting. Neil went out to check the stage call and came back to announce they were on.

The screams and chantings of the audience filtered down the glossy cream corridors leading from the dressing room to the stage. I went ahead of the Beatles and slipped through a curtained door into the auditorium. The screams became more insistent when the compère started to announce the Beatles. Then the curtains swept back and they were lit up by the spotlights: Ringo climbed behind his set of drums raised at the back of the stage and beamed his sunny smile; George fingered his guitar and grinned at the audience; Paul calmly took the microphone and waited for the noise to subside. As he began his introduction, John broke into jerky motions at the other end of the stage to loosen up the show. Paul announced the first number and they bounced straight into it through the screamed response from the fans: 'Long Tall Sally'.

What gave the shine to the Beatles that night and through the following years was the freshness of their music, their enthusiasm and sense of fun, and especially their easy rapport with the audience through their songs. I had the pleasure of experiencing this phenomenon as I travelled with them along the coast to Southampton for a TV appearance, attended other concerts, spent time with them in and around the hotel taking informal pictures and got to know them both as individuals and as musicians in a group.

At some stage during the tour, Brian Epstein mentioned they were working on an album to be released at the end of the year and would be needing a cover picture. I suggested a black-and-white photograph, which seemed an appropriate way to reflect the image of the Beatles in black. The boys liked the idea and the session was set up for noon the following day in the hotel dining room. The large windows let in a bright sidelight and the dark maroon velvet curtains were pulled round as a backdrop. Neil had the job of getting the Beatles up on time and making sure they all had the right clothes. We decided to use the black turtleneck sweaters, which they wore at the time, to keep the picture simple. I don't remember consciously arranging the Beatles in any particular order, but noticed later that what we ended up with on the cover of 'With The Beatles' (in America, 'Meet The Beatles') was the reverse order of their grouping on their first album cover 'Please Please Me'.

The Beatles were pleased with the results and, although there was resistance from EMI to using a black-and-white photograph, both George Martin, their record producer, and Brian Epstein felt strongly that a black-and-white image was right, they had their way. Black-and-white photographs had been used for jazz album covers, whose standards of design were consistently high, but it was the first time, to my knowledge, that a black-and-white photograph had been used on an LP cover for popular musicians. Up to that time and until the filming of *Help!* (with the exception of the 'Beatles For Sale' cover) I took only black-and-white photographs of the Beatles.

Between other professional assignments I continued to take photographs of the Beatles on a freelance basis, mostly at Abbey Road – a complex of cavernous recording studios. The walls of the studio were lined with faded pegboard and padded cloth covered with a wire mesh. The neons high in the ceiling cast a cold, flat light on the entangled wires, amplifiers, microphones and musicians. In this atmosphere, sunny songs like 'Can't Buy Me Love' were recorded. The Beatles' songs and arrangements were arrived at from lyrics scribbled on scraps of paper, through play and replay, through mixes and remixes, and were recorded into the early hours of the morning. Brian had a knack of arriving at a time when everyone wanted a fresh ear to listen to the mix of a song. He would either nod his pleased approval or diplomatically make suggestions for changes. Neil Aspinall and Mal Evans, the road managers, kept the cups of tea flowing and sandwiches supplied, fielding calls from eager girls and keen reporters, fixing guitar strings, amps and drums. The long hours spent recording were interrupted by trips to their tailors, press interviews and meetings with lawyers, agents and accountants – sometimes in unlikely places such as London Zoo, which was near the studios and had a quiet cafeteria during the winter months.

The bright lights of the stage made a welcome change. On 13 October 1963 the Beatles topped the bill at the London Palladium; the show went out live on TV and was watched by an estimated 15,000,000 viewers. At a prestige appearance at the Prince of Wales Theatre on 4 November, the Beatles were billed alongside Marlene Dietrich for a Royal Variety Show attended by British royalty, and transmitted live by television to the nation. 'Rattle your jewels and

9

clap your hands,' was John's irreverent command to the audience. The infectious enthusiasm of the Beatles and the bounce with which they performed captivated the audience who on this occasion were not teenage fans but people who could afford the high-priced tickets and had come to hear Marlene Dietrich sing her sultry songs. While the Beatles swept their way into the hearts of middle England, Marlene Dietrich, clad in skintight glitter, drank backstage to the songs of yesterday.

The Beatles began to enjoy their success in an increasingly swinging London. Their singles were topping the charts, the media were buzzing with coverage of them, and London showbiz was happy to see them at its parties. In the late hours, after the parties, the Beatles would disperse to their preferred night haunts, though mostly their favourite was the Ad Lib in Soho, a club jammed with local and international nightlifers in jeans and dinner jackets. A fine Jamaican chef called Winston would come dancing out of the kitchen waving a tambourine to loosen up the clubbers. I remember some vivid juxtapositions on the softly lit banquettes – Ringo Starr and Tony Bennett, John Lennon and Judy Garland. Photographers, writers, designers, playboys and playgirls mingled with stars like Steve McQueen, Marlon Brando, Roman Polanski and Catherine Deneuve. On the crowded dance floor they hully-gullied, hitch-hiked, wully-bullied and watusied the night away.

Sometimes Brian Epstein would come along to have some fun with the boys, but mostly he had his own nightlife. For managerial and promotional reasons he encouraged the Beatles to move to London. Ringo and George shared an apartment in Mayfair, Paul moved in with his girlfriend, Jane Asher, while John and Cynthia and their young son Julian took an apartment above mine at 13 Emperor's Gate, Kensington.

With the temptations of sudden success and the big-city life, being a married Beatle was not easy for John. In the early days his marriage was kept under wraps to enhance his appeal to the fans, and this created pressures on both him and Cynthia. He would come home at the end of a day of meetings, recordings, performances and interviews, and slump down in front of the TV, accepting in his numbed state the patient attention of his wife, or the playful demands of his son. His character oscillated between extremes of shyness and frivolity, arrogance and humility.

After the success of the Beatles' first English tour, and with the Palladium and other TV shows behind them, Brian wanted to take the group to Europe before venturing to America, on which he had set his sights. I accompanied them on a five-day trip to Sweden, where because of the hotel room shortage I had to share a room with John. He commented dryly on the lack of silken-haired blondes amongst the fans — he hadn't expected so many brunettes or boys. But it was a quick, cold visit — no time for 'Norwegian Wood'.

In January 1964 we visited Paris. The Beatles enjoyed the luxury of a suite at the elegant George v Hotel, and their black boots and snappy suits contrasted with the pale marble walls of the lobby with its chandelier-lit, stuccoed ceilings. Around the corner from the hotel was the Blue Note Club, where jazz pianist Bud Powell was playing. The Beatles dropped in, met Powell and sat sipping Scotch and Coke, listening to his music. But it was another world of music to which they belonged; their show for the Parisians was at the Olympia Theatre on the same bill as Sylvie Vartin. 'Mersey Beaucoup' was John's way of acknowledging the rousing reception from the audience.

On these trips the Beatles were loaded with cameras and when photographed in the Champs-Elysées by the French press they were carrying as much equipment as some of the pros. Although a working visit, it soon took on the atmosphere of a holiday. Because of their fame and the consequent attention and curiosity of the public, their street appearances became spontaneous theatre. They were quick to capitalize on these encounters and turn them into vivid publicity.

The end of 1963 had been a busy time for John. He had signed a contract to do a book, *In His Own Write*. The surreal wit which he expressed in his drawings and writings, done at his own whim, had suddenly become a professional commitment. John was a musician at heart, as well as very much a last-minute man, and he needed a lot of urging from his publisher to complete the book. I had been asked to design it, and we spent many hours in my flat shuffling through the drawings to find ones which were most relevant to the stories and poems. John enjoyed the disciplined and personal nature of the work — it was a complete contrast to the world of the Beatles. We would take breaks to listen to music; he introduced me to some American groups, while I tried to see if the music of Charlie Parker or Coltrane had any interest for him. I played a recording of some 'musique concrète' by the French composer Pierre Henri, and an album of electronic sounds which intrigued him with their strangeness. But rock and roll and rhythm and blues were what he really liked.

After Christmas, John came back from a family visit to Liverpool and prepared with the others for the trip to America. The Beatles were in tune with America through the music of the Shirelles, the Miracles, the Ronettes, Buddy Holly, Bob Dylan, Elvis Presley, Chuck Berry, James Brown, Bo Diddley, Mary Wells, Major Lance, the Drifters, the Coasters, the Crickets and a host of others. They flew out of London's Heathrow Airport on the morning of 7 February; from the steps of their plane, looking back at the terminal building, they waved to layer upon layer of fans, officials and press. Buoyed by this send-off they winged their way to the glitter of New York and came down the steps of their plane to an even greater response. En route they had the company of the legendary American record producer, Phil Spector, whose curved sunglasses made him look like the living embodiment of New York nightlife.

After an impromptu press conference at the Pan Am terminal building, where rapid questions were fielded with ease, the Beatles were hustled into black limousines and driven through the outskirts of the city, through Harlem and downtown to the luxury of the Plaza Hotel. The hotel would never have accepted the reservations had they known the trouble that was in store: liveried doormen had to check the sudden surges of young girls towards the revolving entrance doors, security men on the floor of the suite allocated to the Beatles discovered fans climbing up the drainpipes, and the hotel switchboard was flooded with incoming calls.

Murray the K, the celebrated New York disc jockey, had plugged the Beatles' music on the New York airwaves before their arrival, so it was natural that he be accorded space in the immediate entourage. From day one he was right there, in their rooms and on the road: 'What's happening, baby? The Beatles are what's happening – tonight and every night on WINS', he would chant into his portable recorder. Other media responded eagerly, and press conferences were arranged in the hotel on a rotating basis. At one, for the editors of teen magazines, John was asked if there were any performers in his family. With a deadpan expression he replied, 'Only my father and mother.'

Tom Wolfe wrote up their arrival for the *Herald Tribune*, and *Look* and *Life* magazines vied for exclusive cover stories. At a party given by the photographer Mel Sokolsky, a young Ali McGraw confided to me that her friend, the writer Gloria Steinem, wanted to interview John for a New York magazine. They met in a motel room near La Guardia Airport, where a clandestine meeting had also been been arranged with Bob Dylan, before the Beatles took off for Miami. There were also hopes for a meeting with Elvis Presley. When they arrived in America, the Beatles received a telegram from Elvis welcoming them to the States and complimenting them on their album cover for 'Meet The Beatles'. The Beatles, especially Paul, wanted to meet 'the King', but the crowded schedule made it impossible.

Police on horseback kept the crowds at bay when the Beatles arrived at the CBS studio in New York for 'The Ed Sullivan Show'. The suite at the Plaza Hotel had a constant flow of visitors, among them Phil Spector, the Ronettes, top brass from Capitol Records, concert promoters, and a rep from Pepsi-Cola who presented the Beatles with four radios in the shape of Pepsi-Cola dispensers with sockets for earplug extensions. When the Beatles were invited to lunch at the exclusive '21' club, they caused a stir by walking in clutching their switched-on Pepsi radios.

Eager to catch some of the New York nightlife, they made it to the Peppermint Lounge to see Joey Dee and the Starlighters, who, with nimble footwork, did the Peppermint Twist around the tiny stage. Then, with a chorus of 'You do it like this', they jumped together on to a rail separating the stage from the audience – still twisting. It was a super-sharp American showbiz act, 'tight and bright' as they say in New York. Next stop was the Wagon Wheel, to see Goldie and the Gingerbreads, an all-girl band wearing glittering skintight costumes.

The Beatles took the train to Washington, D.C., for their one performance at the Washington Coliseum. A whole railroad car was set aside so that the press and television could indulge in a media carnival of clicking cameras, zooming lenses and angled microphones. The Beatles posed and wisecracked as the train sped along. A quick change at their hotel in Washington, then onstage at the Coliseum to a rapturous response from the packed audience, back to the hotel for a shower and on to the British Embassy for a reception in their honour. Next day, back to New York for two concerts at Carnegie Hall, then off to Miami.

The sun shone in Miami, making a welcome break from the slushy snow of New York. Rooms had been booked for the Beatles at Ed Sullivan's Deauville Hotel, but accommodations were so tight that George Harrison had to share a room with Murray the K. After their performance on 'The Ed Sullivan Show', watched by an estimated 75,000,000 Americans, the Beatles took a day's break before their return to London. As the Beatles relaxed at a beachside house with its own pool, Paul was approached by a heavily-built figure in shades who said he could arrange a special concession for their songs on jukeboxes in Detroit and Chicago. Paul feigned innocence at the suggestion.

A last encounter, a few miles away, was with Cassius Clay, the world heavy-weight boxing champion, who interrupted his intensive workout to meet the Beatles for a publicity stunt. The four lads lined up in the ring opposite the 'Louisville Lip', with their fists raised. Cassius beat his chest and insisted that, though the Beatles were the prettiest, he was the greatest. No one else in America had confronted the Beatles with such arrogance and panache; Clay's ego seemed as big as those of the four Beatles put together. But once out of the ring and back in his dressing room, he dealt patiently with the crush of reporters.

When they were leaving America the Beatles were asked how they found the country. 'We went to Greenland and turned left,' was the instant response.

Their wit and their music had created waves of excitement across the continent. For the first time, the American public had taken a group of popular English musicians to its heart. The Beatles had conquered America.

Soon after their return to England, in March 1964, the Beatles began filming *A Hard Day's Night*, directed by Richard Lester. Since the production was based at Twickenham Film Studios, and all the exterior locations were in that area, the Beatles had a chance to consolidate their lives for a time without too much moving around. The film was shot in the spirit of an improvised home movie; in this way, Lester was able to mix, in a spontaneous fashion, the raw talents of the four musicians with the skills of professional actors. He was adept at this kind of improvisation and the gamble paid off — the film proved to be a critical and box-office success.

The Beatles enjoyed the communal atmosphere of filming and the technology of cameras and lights. The shooting schedule was tight — the film was completed in less than two months — and this introduced the Beatles to a new discipline: that of getting up early. The romance on set was provided by George Harrison and Pattie Boyd, who had a small role in the film. They married in January 1966.

Like the film, the year 1964 moved along at a fast pace. John had success with his book, *In His Own Write*, while the release of the film together with the soundtrack album, gave fresh impetus to the Beatles' careers. Their new singles instantly topped the charts. The Beatles celebrated their success; they bought houses and cars, went abroad for holidays. Then, with summer over, it was time to think of an album for Christmas. Appropriately titled 'Beatles For Sale', it contained one song that summed up the busy year: 'Eight Days A Week'. On a wintry day in London's Hyde Park, I photographed the Beatles in colour for the front and back of the album. Inside the album I used two pictures that celebrated highlights of the year: the Beatles in concert at the Coliseum in Washington, D.C., and during the filming of *A Hard Day's Night*.

In the early months of 1965, preparations began for the filming of *Help!* The production was based at the Twickenham Studios, but this time it was to be shot in colour, with a budget that allowed for locations in the Alps and the Bahamas. The comic-strip scenario was again directed by Richard Lester; I worked on the production as colour consultant and title designer. After the freezing locations in Austria, it was a pleasure to climb aboard a chartered plane bound for the Bahamas.

The presence of the Beatles in this Caribbean paradise made a great impression on the American tourists as well as on the local community. On one occasion Ringo was approached in a Nassau street by a blue-rinsed American lady who asked, 'And which one are you?' 'Sammy Davis, Jr.' was Ringo's jaunty reply. Seemingly satisfied, she took a quick snapshot and moved on.

The importance of the production was underlined by the visit of top executives from United Artists. They reviewed the progress of the filming like gods reviewing the course of destiny, but with little power to affect the result. The film had its own style and momentum, and everyone beavered away, in the sea and on the sand, to create a colourful comedy, while evenings were spent in the funky Nassau clubs. The Beatles, having left their ladies at home, shared a large villa near the beach; once again, for a short spell, they were together as a close-knit group.

The production was completed in London with elaborate sets built in the studio. For the end title sequence I filmed the Beatles and other members of the cast using kaleidoscopic camera techniques to create the impression of a world inside Ringo's ring. For the design of the album cover I had the Beatles signalling in semaphore the word HELP!

While the film was being shaped in the editing room, the Beatles were shaping their domestic lives. John had moved into a large house on the St George's Hill estate in Weybridge, an hour's drive from London. Ringo and Maureen, married in 1965, moved to a house on the same estate, while not far away, near Esher, George had found a well-designed modern bungalow with a swimming pool, surrounded by a high brick wall. After years of public exposure they wanted privacy and a place to call home. The uniform image of the fabulous foursome was dissolving into a loose association of four individuals.

It was becoming very difficult to get the four together for a photo session. The photograph for 'Rubber Soul', the last album cover in which I was involved, was taken in the garden of John's house in Weybridge — the central point for three of them. Paul drove down from London. The distorted effect in the photo was a reflection of the changing shape of their lives. They had begun their careers as musicians, but the wide range of people and ideas that they had encountered, their financial success, and the new privacy of their homes encouraged them to take up more varied and personal interests. As a group they were still the Beatles, but as individuals they were experiencing a subtle chemistry of change. The direction in which they were moving was inwards.

All this was yesterday. And tomorrow? As Ringo once said, 'Tomorrow never knows.'

ROBERT FREEMAN   15

Ringo in his room at the President Hotel, London,
during the Beatles' first English tour, 1963.
OPPOSITE The Beatles, Southern Television Studios, 1963.

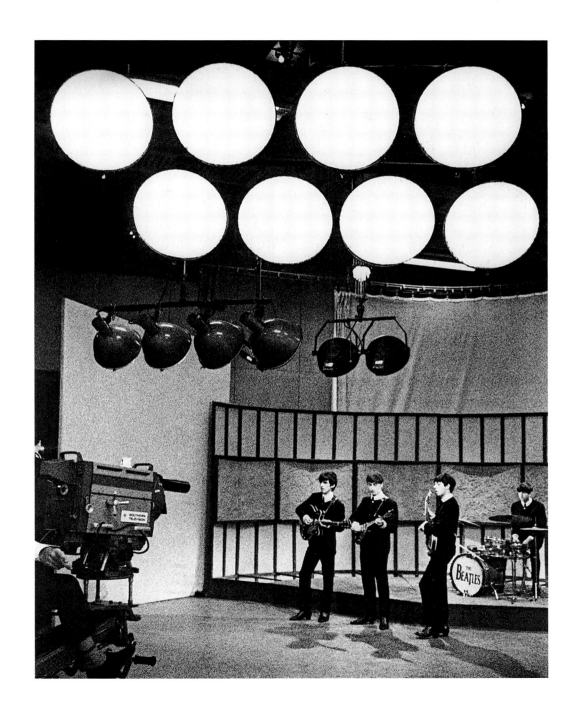

18

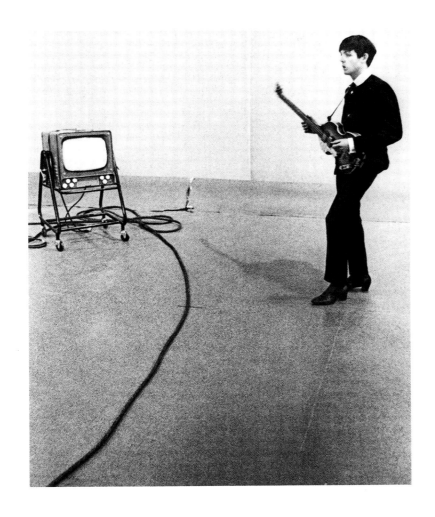

Paul waits for a stage call by a TV monitor.
OPPOSITE John on a TV screen during the Beatles'
Southern Television appearance.

John rehearses with Paul for a TV show. The Soho suits by Dougie
Millings were uniform for the Beatles' stage and TV shows in 1963.

John in the dressing room of a Birmingham theatre.

George Harrison backstage.

George Harrison.

24

Ringo in the dressing room of a Bournemouth theatre. He seemed
happiest onstage or in the clubs; in between was just waiting.
OPPOSITE Ringo Starr.

25

Paul reads a letter from a fan. He would shuffle through wads of
envelopes and find the liveliest extracts to read out to the others.
OPPOSITE Paul shams the strain of signing autographs.

26

27

OPPOSITE   Passing the time in a hotel lounge during their
successful first English tour, the rising stars of popular music,
John, George and Ringo, scan the newspapers for the charts and
the reviews. Outside, the fans (ABOVE) wait patiently.

30   Paul and (OPPOSITE) George with fans, Bournemouth.

Neil Aspinall, the Beatles' road manager, carries
their guitars to the stage door of the Albert Hall.

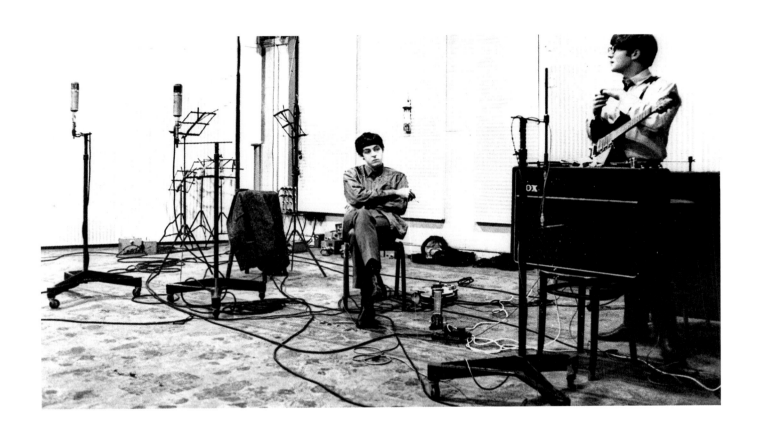

Paul and John. Abbey Road Studios. 41

42

Paul and (OPPOSITE) John. Abbey Road Studios.

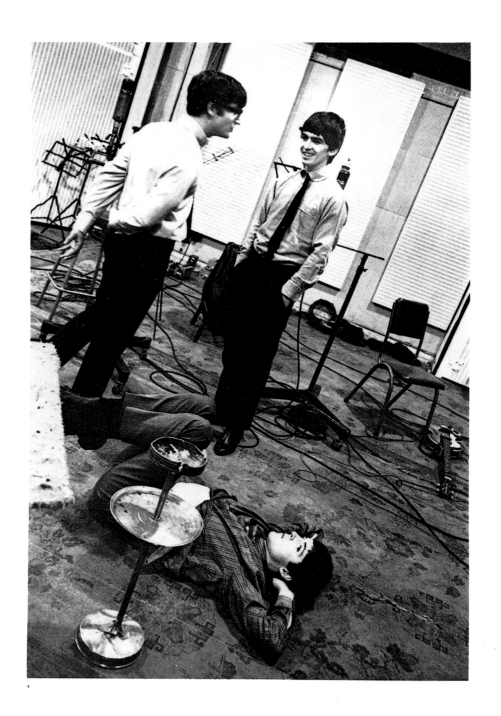

Ringo Starr, Abbey Road Studios.
OPPOSITE Paul takes a break during the recording
of the album 'With The Beatles', 1963.

46

Ringo and Paul outside London Zoo. The Beatles sometimes
ate in the zoo's cafeteria since it is near the Abbey Road
Studios and quiet during the winter months.
OPPOSITE Paul McCartney.

47

The Beatles pose before a mural in the lobby of Twickenham Film
Studios' viewing theatre, where they watched the 'rushes' of
A Hard Day's Night with the director, Richard Lester, 1964.
OPPOSITE Brian Epstein, the Beatles' manager, sits for his portrait
in an armchair in Liberty's department store, London.

On location for *A Hard Day's Night*: fans at Marylebone Station
pursue the Beatles into the entrance hall and on to the train.

Ringo, John and George filming *A Hard Day's Night*.

Richard Lester (left) shows his good humour directing a scene with
Paul and Victor Spinetti (right). Situations were often improvised
to create spontaneity in the action and dialogue.

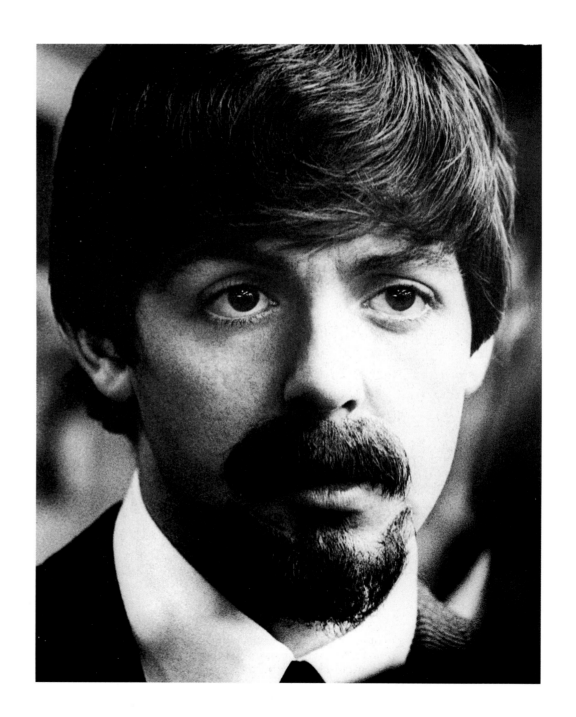

54

John poses in one of his disguises from *Help!* for a profile in *The Sunday Times* colour magazine. He enjoyed the circus atmosphere of filming, contributing to it on one occasion by driving to the studio in his brand-new Ferrari with 'learner' plates on.
OPPOSITE Paul in disguise to escape the attention of the fans.

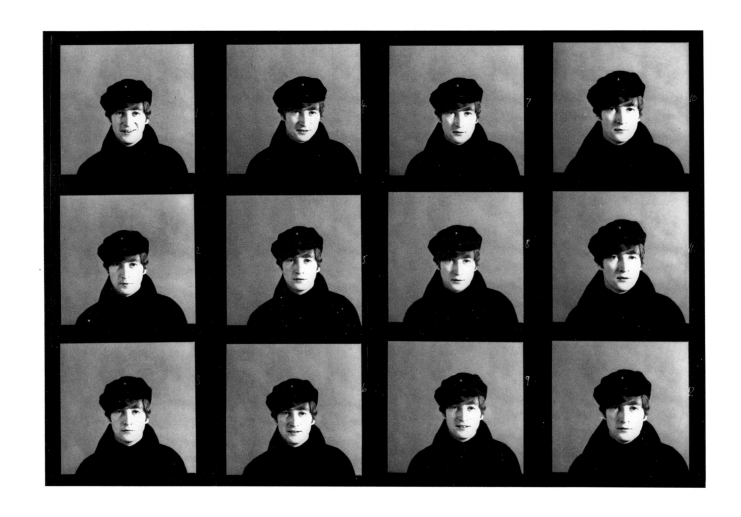

Contact sheet from the photo session for the cover of John's book
In His Own Write. John was nervous about having his whimsical
drawings and writings published, and at the literary luncheon held
in his honour by Foyle's bookshop he could muster only a one-line
speech: 'Thank you, you've got a lucky face.' 1964.

56

John Lennon.

OPPOSITE AND ABOVE The entrance to John's first London home –
Flat 3. 13 Emperor's Gate. Kensington. Although he used the
pseudonym Hadley. the comings and goings of large limousines
made his home conspicuous. and the fans soon found him out.

59

Paul poses with the New York disc jockey Murray the K, whose
enthusiasm for the Beatles kept him close to the action during the
hectic days in New York; he would record his reports from hotel
rooms, elevators, corridors and cars.
OPPOSITE The Beatles departure for their first American tour was
sensational: fans crowded every available viewpoint at the terminal
building at Heathrow Airport to scream, shout and wave farewell.
It was a moment of triumph for Brian Epstein (just visible behind Ringo).

The Beatles performing at the Washington Coliseum,
Washington D.C. on 11 February, 1964.

The Beatles arrived in New York to a tremendous welcome from
their American fans and the jostling attention of press and television.

Ringo with his wife, Maureen, and their parents at his wedding at
Caxton Hall. In the back row are Cynthia and John Lennon,
George Harrison and Brian Epstein. 1965.

Brian Epstein was best man at Ringo's wedding. In the reception
room at Caxton Hall he jokes with a nervous Ringo while they wait
for the bride to arrive. The event was kept secret from the fans,
and the news only broke that evening in the papers.

ABOVE AND OPPOSITE Paul McCartney.

68

Ringo looks out over London from a window in the house of the
film columnist Peter Noble.

OPPOSITE John stands behind a suit of armour in the entrance hall
of his new house on an exclusive estate in Weybridge, part of
London's 'stockbroker belt'. A designer friend of Brian Epstein
supervised the interior decoration; working on short notice, he had
the delicate task of fusing his own taste with that of the forthright
but whimsical John and the more home-loving Cynthia. 1965.

John converted one room on the top floor of his Weybridge house
into a painting studio. There, in his quieter moments, he would
indulge himself with thick applications of oil to canvas.

70

George by a lake near his Esher home. A few days before, he had
bought a beautiful Aston Martin, which had to be returned almost
immediately for repainting when he discovered to his dismay that
an oil leak from the front wheel hub had spilt on to the paintwork.

71

72

ABOVE AND OPPOSITE George Harrison.

74   Paul McCartney.

Ringo Starr.

The Beatles photographed in London's Hyde Park
for the 'Beatles For Sale' album, 1964.

John poses with a panda in the bedroom of his Weybridge
house for the American magazine *McCall's*, 1965.

The Beatles' success gave them access to more technology and longer hours at the studios. The songs for 'Rubber Soul' were recorded under the glare of neon lights high in the ceiling of the cavernous studio. amid the tangle of wires and equipment. For technical reasons Ringo (OPPOSITE) and his drums were kept at some distance from the others during recordings. 1965.

80   John Lennon.

Malcolm Evans, the Beatles' assistant road manager,
waits with Ringo during a long recording session.
His gentle, buffoon-like manner made him frequently
the butt of the Beatles' irreverent humour.
OPPOSITE Paul McCartney.

Ringo watches from behind the plate glass
of the mixing room, Abbey Road Studios.
opposite George Martin holds a horn to his head during the
recording of 'Rubber Soul'. With his musical sense and technical
ability, gentleman George was a patient producer of the songs and
sounds of the Beatles. He had already recorded five albums with
the group: 'Please Please Me', 'With The Beatles', 'A Hard Day's
Night', 'Beatles For Sale' and 'Help!'.

Dressed in the costumes of a Tyrolean band, the Beatles perform
for the filming of *Help!* in the Austrian Alps, 1965.

Clenching a machete between his teeth, John comes
to grips with actor Patrick Cargill on Paradise
Island in the Bahamas for the final scene of the film.

George up to his neck filming *Help!*

Ringo, the sacrificial victim in the *Help!* scenario,
waits for action in the water on Paradise Island.

The Beatles in the final scene of *Help!*

The shadow of the Deauville Hotel falls across the
sands of Miami Beach. where the fans wait to catch a
glimpse of the four musicians from Liverpool. 1964.

MAIN EVENTS IN THE BEATLES' CAREERS, 1963-5

1963

February	Tour of Britain with Helen Shapiro
2 March	A Beatles' single, 'Please Please Me', tops the *Melody Maker*'s charts for the first time
22 March	First LP album, 'Please Please Me', released
March–May	Tour of Britain with Chris Montez and Tommy Roe
May–October	First tour of Britain as top of the bill
23 August	Final concert at the Cavern Club, Liverpool
13 October	Sunday Night at the London Palladium, broadcast live on TV
24–29 October	Tour of Sweden
November–December	Tour of Britain
4 November	Royal Variety Performance, Prince of Wales Theatre, London
14 December	Southern Fan Club Convention, Wimbledon Palais
21 December	Christmas show at the Bradford Gaumont
22 December	Christmas show at the Liverpool Empire
24 December–11 January 1964	Christmas shows at Finsbury Park Astoria Theatre, London

1964

16 January–4 February	Olympia Theatre, Paris
February	First tour of USA
9 February	'The Ed Sullivan Show'. Beatles' first live appearance on American TV
11 February	Concert at the Washington Coliseum. Washington, D.C.
12 February	Two concerts at Carnegie Hall, New York
16 February	'The Ed Sullivan Show' live from Miami
March–April	Filming *A Hard Day's Night*
April–May	Tour of Britain
26 April	New Musical Express Poll Winners Concert, Wembley Stadium, London
31 May	Pops Alive, Prince of Wales Theatre, London
June–August	Tour of Hong Kong, Denmark, Australia, New Zealand, Sweden and Britain
6 July	Première of *A Hard Day's Night* at the London Pavilion. 'A Hard Day's Night' LP released
23 July	Night of 100 Stars (charity show), London Palladium
August–September	American tour
23 August	Concert at Shea Stadium, New York
October–November	British tour
December	'Beatles For Sale' LP released
24 December–16 January 1965	Christmas shows at the Hammersmith Odeon, London

1965

February–April	Filming *Help!*
11 April	New Musical Express Poll Winners Concert, Wembley Stadium
June–July	Tour of France, Italy and Spain
29 July	Première of *Help!* at London Pavilion. 'Help!' LP released
December	'Rubber Soul' LP released
December	British tour